Rudest

‹ place names

by Stewart Ferris
and Alastair Williams

Crombie Jardine
PUBLISHING LIMITED
13 Nonsuch Walk, Cheam, Surrey, SM2 7LG
www.crombiejardine.com

This edition was first published by
Crombie Jardine Publishing Limited in 2005

ISBN 1-905102-48-8

Written and designed by
Stewart Ferris and Alastair Williams

Printed and bound in the United Kingdom by
William Clowes Ltd, Beccles, Suffolk

Contents

BOTTOM BURN

BOTTOMS (REAR)

Auchtertool
Fife
Scotland

4

BOTTOM FLASH

Winsford
Cheshire
England

BOTTOMS

BOTTOMS (REAR)

**West Yorkshire
England**

BOTTOMS (REAR)

BULLYHOLE BOTTOM

**Gaerllwyd
Monmouthshire
Wales**

7

BOTTOMS (REAR)

BURNT BOTTOM

Beaminster
Dorset
England

BUSHY BOTTOM

**Edburton
West Sussex
England**

9

BUTTOCK

BOTTOMS (REAR)

**Barley
Lancashire
England**

10

BOTTOMS (REAR)

BUTTOCK POINT

>

Bute
Argyll and Bute
Scotland

BOTTOMS (REAR)

DIRTY
GUTTER

**Bottom House
Leek
Staffordshire
England**

BOTTOMS (REAR)

HARD CRAG

**Haverthwaite
Cumbria
England**

HERBERT'S HOLE

BOTTOMS (REAR)

Chesham
Buckinghamshire
England

HOLE BOTTOM

**Todmorden
West Yorkshire
England**

15

LICKEY END

BOTTOMS (REAR)

**Bromsgrove
West Midlands
England**

16

LICKHAM BOTTOM

Hemyock
Cullompton
Devon
England

17

BOTTOMS (REAR)

LOOSE BOTTOM

**Falmer
West Sussex
England**

PETT BOTTOM

**Stowting
Kent
England**

19

PRATT'S BOTTOM

BOTTOMS (REAR)

Kent
England

20

BOTTOMS (REAR)

ROTTEN BOTTOM

Meggethead
Scottish Borders
Scotland

21

SCRATCHY BOTTOM

BOTTOMS (REAR)

**Lulworth
Dorset
England**

FEMALE FRONT BOTTOMS

BEAVER GREEN

**Ashford
Kent
England**

BUSHY BOTTOM

FEMALE FRONT BOTTOMS

**Fulking
West Sussex
England**

24

CLITSOME FARM

**Washford
Somerset
England**

25

COULTER-FANNY

FEMALE FRONT BOTTOMS

**Fraserburgh
Aberdeenshire
Scotland**

FEMALE FRONT BOTTOMS

LADY'S HOLE

**Beadnell
Northumberland
England**

27

FEMALE FRONT BOTTOMS

MINGES

**Widford
Hertfordshire
England**

FEMALE FRONT BOTTOMS

TWATT

**Orkney
Scotland**

29

TWATHATS

FEMALE FRONT BOTTOMS

**Ruthwell Parish
Dumfriesshire
Scotland**

MALE FRONT BOTTOMS

BALLS CROSS

>

**Petworth
West Sussex
England**

MALE FRONT BOTTOMS

BELL END

Worcestershire
England

32

MALE FRONT BOTTOMS

BULLOCK DOWN

**Beachy Head
East Sussex
England**

COCK ALLEY

MALE FRONT BOTTOMS

**Chesterfield
Derbyshire
England**

COCK BRIDGE

MALE FRONT BOTTOMS

Aberdeen
Aberdeenshire
Scotland

35

COCK HEADS

MALE FRONT BOTTOMS

**North York Moors
National Park
North Yorkshire
England**

36

MALE FRONT BOTTOMS

COCK PEN

**Midlothian
Scotland**

37

MALE FRONT BOTTOMS

COCKING

Chichester
West Sussex
England

MALE FRONT BOTTOMS

COCKS

**Bolingey
Cornwall
England**

MALE FRONT BOTTOMS

CUCKOO'S KNOB

**Pewsey
Wiltshire
England**

40

MALE FRONT BOTTOMS

DANCING DICKS

**Witham
Essex
England**

41

DICK SLACK

MALE FRONT BOTTOMS

**Rishworth Moor
West Yorkshire
England**

MALE FRONT BOTTOMS

GREAT COCKUP

**Bassenthwaite
Cumbria
England**

43

KNOB HILL

MALE FRONT BOTTOMS

Warnham
West Sussex
England

44

Britain's RUDEST place names

MALE FRONT BOTTOMS

LITTLE COCKUP

**Bassenthwaite
Cumbria
England**

45

LORD HEREFORD'S KNOB

MALE FRONT BOTTOMS

Twmpa
Powys
Wales

46

MALE FRONT BOTTOMS

NACKER HOLE

**Beadnell
Northumberland
England**

47

NOB END

MALE FRONT BOTTOMS

**Little Lever
Greater Manchester
England**

MALE FRONT BOTTOMS

PENISHAPE-NTRE

Llanspyddid
Powys
Wales

MALE FRONT BOTTOMS

PENISTONE

**South Yorkshire
England**

50

MALE FRONT BOTTOMS

PRICK-WILLOW

Ely
Cambridgeshire
England

RANDY PIKE

MALE FRONT BOTTOMS

**Wray Castle
Cumbria
England**

52

MALE FRONT BOTTOMS

SANDY BALLS

**Fordingbridge
Hampshire
England**

SHAFTEN-HOE END

MALE FRONT BOTTOMS

Royston
Hertfordshire
England

MALE FRONT BOTTOMS

UPPER DICKER

**Hailsham
East Sussex
England**

MALE FRONT BOTTOMS

WILLEY

Warwickshire
England

MALE FRONT BOTTOMS

WILLY KNOT

**Branthwaite
Cumbria
England**

BOOBY DINGLE

KNOCKERS

Peterchurch
Herefordshire
England

KNOCKERS

BREASTY HAW

Satterthwaite
Cumbria
England

TITMORE GREEN

KNOCKERS

**Stevenage
Hertfordshire
England**

60

KNOCKERS

TITSON

**Bude
Cornwall
England**

61

Britain's Rudest place names

TITTY HILL

KNOCKERS

**Midhurst
West Sussex
England**

62

TYTTEN-HANGER →

**St Albans
Hertfordshire
England**

UPPER LADY MEADOWS

KNOCKERS

Leek Staffordshire England

Britain's **Rudest** place names

OOER MISSUS!

BONKLE

North Lanarkshire
Scotland

DICKEN DYKE

OOER MISSUS!

Harrogate
North Yorkshire
England

OOER MISSUS!

GIRDLE FELL

>

**Byrness
Northumberland
England**

Britain's **Rudest** place names

LICKFOLD

OOER MISSUS!

**West Sussex
England**

OOER MISSUS!

THREE HOLES

Downham Market
Norfolk
England

THREE
LEG
CROSS

OOER MISSUS!

Ticehurst
East Sussex
England

70

OOER MISSUS!

WETWANG

**East Riding of
Yorkshire
England**

FULKING HILL

SHAGGING

Fulking
West Sussex
England

72

SHAGGS

**East Lulworth
Dorset
England**

RUG MUNCHING AND LOLLIPOP LICKING

**COCKLICK
END**

Slaidburn
Lancashire
England

74

LICKEY END

**Bromsgrove
Worcestershire
England**

RUG MUNCHING AND LOLLIPOP LICKING

TONGUE OF GANGSTA

**Kirkwall
Orkney Islands
Scotland**

MONKEY SPANKING

COCK PLAY

**Bewcastle
Cumbria
England**

77

GREAT TOSSON

MONKEY SPANKING

Rothbury
Northumberland
England

MONKEY SPANKING

HANDCOCK'S BOTTOM

**Blandford Forum
Dorset
England**

Britain's Rudest place names

TOSSIDE

MONKEY SPANKING

**North Yorkshire
England**

80

MONKEY SPANKING

TUGFORD

**Shropshire
England**

REAR ADMIRALS AND MUFF DIVERS

BROWN WILLY

**Bodmin Moor
Cornwall
England**

82

BUMMERS HILL

**Little Hormead
Hertfordshire
England**

REAR ADMIRALS AND MUFF DIVERS

COCKER-MOUTH

**Cumbria
England**

REAR ADMIRALS AND MUFF DIVERS

DEVIL'S DYKE

**Poynings
West Sussex
England**

REAR ADMIRALS AND MUFF DIVERS

DYKE

**Bourne
Lincolnshire
England**

86

REAR ADMIRALS AND MUFF DIVERS

DYKEHEAD

**North Lanarkshire
Scotland**

REAR ADMIRALS AND MUFF DIVERS

GAY STREET

**Pulborough
West Sussex
England**

HOLE OF BUGARS

Lerwick
Shetland Islands
Scotland

REAR ADMIRALS AND MUFF DIVERS

PUMP-BOTTOM FARM

Chichester
West Sussex
England

90

RING BURN

**Glenwhilly
Dumfries and
Galloway
Scotland**

REAR ADMIRALS AND MUFF DIVERS

SODOM

**Denbighshire
Wales**

THREE COCKS

**Powys
Wales**

REAR ADMIRALS AND MUFF DIVERS

UP MUDFORD

Yeovil
Somerset
England

94

WIDE OPEN DYKES

**Scaleby
Cumbria
England**

BODILY FUNCTIONS

BELCH-ALWELL

**Dorset
England**

CRAPHAM DOWN

Eastbourne
East Sussex
England

Britain's **Rudest** place names

◄ CRAPSTONE

BODILY FUNCTIONS

**Plymouth
Devon
England**

BODILY FUNCTIONS

LOWER PILES

**South Brent
Devon
England**

PIDDLE

BODILY FUNCTIONS

**Puddletown
Dorset
England**

PIDDLE BROOK

**Pershore
Worcestershire
England**

PISHILL

BODILY FUNCTIONS

**Oxfordshire
England**

PISSER CLOUGH

**Hebden Bridge
West Yorkshire
England**

SHATTON MOOR

BODILY FUNCTIONS

**Bradwell
Derbyshire
England**

SHIT-LINGTON CRAGS

**Bellingham
Northumberland
England**

105

Britain's **Rudest** place names

BODILY FUNCTIONS

< SHITTLE-HOPE

**Durham
England**

106

SPUNKIE

**Lugton
East Ayrshire
Scotland**

TURDEES

BODILY FUNCTIONS

**Chapelhall
North Lanarkshire
Scotland**

108

Britain's **Rudest** place names

BODILY FUNCTIONS

WYRE PIDDLE

Pershore
Worcestershire
England

THE BASTARD

MISCELLANEOUS

Sheanachie
Argyll and Bute
Scotland

BITCH CRAIG

Mountbenger
Scottish Borders
Scotland

Britain's *Rudest* place names

◀ BITCHFIELD

MISCELLANEOUS

Grantham
Lincolnshire
England

112

CUM HAG WOOD

**Coneysthorpe
North Yorkshire
England**

HAIRY SIDE

MISCELLANEOUS

Barleyhill
Northumberland
England

HOOKER'S FARM

**Hickstead
West Sussex
England**

PANTY HILL

MISCELLANEOUS

Dolfor
Powys
Wales

116

SLAG HILL

**Allenheads
Northumberland
England**

STAINES

MISCELLANEOUS

**Surrey
England**

THONG

**Kent
England**

UPPER-THONG

MISCELLANEOUS

**West Yorkshire
England**

120

**Other humour titles
from Crombie Jardine...**

The world's

Rudest

place names

Stewart Ferris
& Alastair Williams

ISBN 1-905102-49-6, £2.99

Shag

your way to
the top

the real fast track to success

Imah Goer

ISBN 1-905102-17-8, £2.99

Shag

yourself slim

The most enjoyable way to lose weight

Imah Goer

ISBN 1-905102-03-8, £2.99

The Little Book of
Book of
Bling!

chek ma frosted bling, it's drippin wiv gold innit?

LEE BOK

ISBN 1-905102-21-6, £2.99

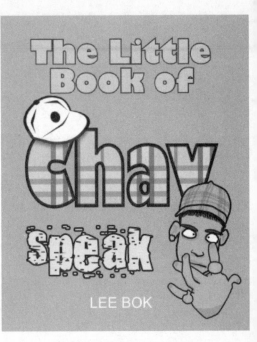

ISBN 1-905102-20-8, £2.99

The Little Book of

Chavs

The Branded Guide to Britain's New Elite

LEE BOK

ISBN 1-905102-01-1, £2.99

All Crombie Jardine books are available from
High Street bookshops, Amazon or Bookpost
(P.O. Box 29, Douglas, Isle of Man, IM99 1BQ.
Tel: 01624 677237, Fax: 01624 670923,
Email: bookshop@enterprise.net.
Postage and packing free within the UK).

www.crombiejardine.com